Afterglow

Moving Beyond the Pain
of Loss and Grief

F. L. Richards

© Copyright 2016, F. L. Richards

All rights reserved.

No part of this book may be reproduced, stored in a retrieval system, or transmitted by any means, electronic, mechanical, photocopying, recording, or otherwise, without written permission from the author.

ISBN: 978-1-60414-930-2

Registered with the Library of Congress

Author's Notes

Except when referencing my partner as co-author, I am intentional about using his real name so that the content of my writing may take on a more personal significance.

Other than scriptural references, statements attributed to the author, or those that are specifically cited, the quotes in the body of this work are taken from the Bereavement Ministry syllabus created by Rev. Anne Atwell, Minister of Connections at Sunshine Cathedral, Ft. Lauderdale, Florida.

Our Journey Together

New York:

Humble beginnings 1986

Puerto Rico:

The view from our terrace 1997

Florida:

Final destination 2001

Dedication

for John

"Where can I go from your presence?
If I go up to the sky, you are there.
If I lay down in the depths, you are there,
If I go beyond the east or live in the
farthest part of the west, you are there.
There is no place apart from you...
for I know you are always with me."
Psalm 139:7-9 (adapted)

Rest, dear one, in the light
of omnipresent love.

Acknowledgments

It is because of the support of many that I have been able to undertake the creation of this work. With heartfelt gratitude, I would like to thank:

John's family and mine for loving us all of these years and demonstrating a beautiful, empowering unity during a time of great sadness in our lives.

Those with whom I am blessed to share the gift of close friendship...Nancy ('Mum'), Rocco, Elaine, Bob and Nancy, Michael and John, Sandy, Jesús and Teri, Charles V, Ada, and Jeannie 'Ish'. Each and together, their presence in my life encourages and sustains me on my path.

The members and friends of Sunshine Cathedral, especially the clergy: Rev. Dr. Durrell Watkins, Rev. Dr. Robert Griffin, Rev. Anne Atwell, Rev. Walt Weiss, Rev. Kevin Tisdol and Rev. Ty Bradley. By nurturing my spiritual growth, they help me to be ever aware of the profound truth that God is with me and all is well.

Dr. Michael Cristiano, whose compassion and professionalism have been instrumental in guiding me away from the pain of loss and grief to a realization that life does go on.

A very special 'thank you' to my dear friend, Nancy Major, for agreeing to transcribe this manuscript. Her spirit of generosity is remarkable.

"The memory of the dead

can indeed outlast

the monuments to the dead."

Living When a Loved One has Died
Earl A. Grollman
"Living Remembrances," p. 107

Contents

	Preface.. xv
I.	A Personal Perspective on Loss and Grief............................3
II.	The Treasure Chest..17
III.	The Present Reality of Time and Place..................................47
IV.	Guideposts... Thoughts and Reflections for the Journey..........................73
	Final Thoughts..81
	A Special Remembrance...84
	About the Author..85
	Other Works..86

Preface

Like a seed in soil, a thought is planted and takes root in consciousness. It begins to grow, relentless in its desire to develop into something more than its beginning and take on form and substance that is tangible. This simple analogy is how the idea to write this book came to be. I knew there would come a time when I would give attention to the seed of inspiration and commence the process of birthing it into something which could be shared with others who might identify with its purpose.

This task could not have been undertaken sooner because the burden of loss and grief rendered me incapable of being ready, willing and able to tend to and nurture that 'seed'. It was ever-present but dormant. For growth to occur, I knew I needed to get out what was inside. That involved getting to a place where I felt grounded and strong enough to express the thoughts and perceptions of my mind and the deep, personal emotions of my heart.

In order to make that movement occur, I needed to develop understandings that would aptly express all that encompassed the experience of loss and grief, then become acquainted with what the idea of forward living was all about. I read several books and became familiar with concepts, definitions, principles and the perceptions of other writers. This was a helpful endeavor, but I began to realize that I needed more because what I had read seemed removed from what I was hoping to uncover as being personally meaningful to those whose works I had investigated. I longed to be able to identify with individuals whose feet were on the same road as mine. I wanted to know that I was not isolated as I walked its path. I yearned to be consoled by sentiments such as, "I have been there," "I know what you are going through," "I understand," so I might hold fast to their strength, comfort and reassurance. It took quite a while, but that intimate connection for which I searched became a reality.

After more than two years, I have come to that place where I am able to recount the experience of loss and grief but not make it a singular or overriding focus. The primary purpose of this book, then, is to celebrate a life shared and a love experienced, indeed, to look back and bask in the afterglow of all that has been while embracing all that continues to be.

As I begin this work, I am reminded of these words:

> *"I will set forth on this journey in hope and trust. What more have I to lose? And how much more to gain!"*
>
> Frank O'Connor

A Personal Perspective

on

Loss and Grief

I

"Deep grief sometimes is like a specific location, a coordinate on the map of time. When you are standing in the forest of sorrow, you cannot imagine that you could ever find your way to a better place. But if someone can assure you that they themselves have stood in that same place, and now have moved on, sometimes this will bring hope."

Elizabeth Gilbert

At different times in our lives, all of us have been cast into the indescribable position of losing someone close to us. Facing the event of death is something we share in common, but the journey which follows is personal and unique. No two of us approach the pain of loss, the process of grief and the task of rebuilding life exactly the same way.

For all who grieve, there are options to consider and decisions to be made. Some people find a fullness of consolation within their circle of family and friends. Those anchors are crucial for them as they search for ways to feel a sense of groundedness in the midst of loss. Others may find it beneficial to seek professional assistance or participate in a bereavement group as they negotiate direction on their journey. Still others, whose lives are rooted in some religious affiliation or are more centered in personal spirituality, look to their belief systems for solace and strength. Even engaging in physical or creative interests may be for some a valuable way to cope with loss. There is no 'right' or 'better' way to grieve. The choice is individual and personal. That is what gives character to the process.

When I lost John, my best friend and partner with whom I shared life, love and learning for twenty eight years, I was faced with a stark reality. This painful, anguish-filled reality was mine alone to experience in ways that were meaningful in my life so I would be able to unscramble and sort out thoughts and emotions which seemed to be racing inside me in so many different directions. It was an unsettling thought to consider that I needed to take ownership of this incredulous occurrence and all that came with it.

In the days after John's passing on January 29, 2014, I found myself surrounded not only by many who had become part of our life in Florida but also by his children...Michael and his wife, Michele, Laurence and his partner, Philip, Caroline, their mom, Linda, his granddaughter, Alora, and brother, Richard. With me also were my children, Jennifer and Brian, my nephew, Jason, and Rocco, my dearest friend of thirty seven years. I held them close to me because the gift of their presence was both vital and valuable. Filled with comfort and reassurance, their words touched my heart. Their actions, all flowing from selfless generosity, reflected a depth of care, concern and compassion I craved at that time. The outpouring of love from John's family was truly remarkable because they, too, had sustained a monumental loss. I wish I had been capable of returning these beautiful gifts to them in more visible ways, but the reality of feeling numb and empty obscured my ability to give as greatly as I received. I was focused inward and just needed to feel safe and protected while facing this unspeakable circumstance.

The viewing was scheduled for Saturday afternoon and evening. I looked to Richard for special support because of his deep spirituality. I trusted that the light of his beautiful spirit would provide strength throughout the weekend. Several brief conversations with him and greeting those who had come to pay respects made those initial hours seem to fly by. As the time for a dinner break neared, Laurence came to me and made the generous offer to take the families and a few close friends for a meal. He wanted to honor his dad's memory by going to a place he knew was meaningful. It had been our favorite eatery. It was large enough to accommodate our number so we might remain together for the in-between hours. A source of temporary distraction from the sadness, that togetherness not only provided for lighter conversation but also served as a reminder of how beautiful was the connection between our families.

The next day, we gathered at my church for a Celebration of Life Service. As emotionally stirring as were the musical selections and readings, the highlight for me was Rev. Durrell's homily. It was all I knew it would be...personally relevant to John and affirming to all who were listening. There was one expression, however, that greatly impacted me. Referring to the moment of his passing, the pastor said "...and God kissed John into eternity." These words were powerful, comforting, reassuring, and fortified me for what remained to be done that day. After the sacrament of communion and final prayer, the more than one hundred in the congregation sang the closing hymn, *Oh God Our Help in Ages Past*. Brian, Jason and John's sons moved slowly to the front to the sanctuary for the purpose of escorting the casket out of the church. I was moved to tears observing the blending of our families in a beautiful moment of unity. My eyes became fixed on my son, Brian, who bore a somber expression, his gaze downward and unwavering. Although I could not presume to know what he was thinking, I so hoped his mind was filled with tender remembrances because John had been a kind, caring, affirming presence in his life.

After arriving at the cemetery a few blocks away, I noticed Linda standing a distance away from where I was seated and motioned to her to join me. As my pastor said the prayer of commendation, she and I held hands in what might be perceived by some as having been an unusual, unlikely moment of closeness. The history of our relationship during my years with John proved otherwise. It was a loud and clear validation that unconditional love is capable of conquering the seeming greatest of challenges.

I realized that the immediate bolstering I had received during these days was temporary because as quickly as those closest to me had arrived from other states, it was time for them to return to their own life responsibilities. Their 'good-byes' ushered in a deadening silence in my home and signaled the need for me to steel myself. Not knowing location or destination, I was about to embark on an inescapable, unknown journey for which I was completely unprepared.

Initially, I thought I would be able to look directly into the eyes of loss and grief and find the strength and courage to go with the flow while trying to avoid being consumed by its powerful grip. That became a tall task, greater than anything I might have imagined. Confrontation manifested itself in a number of ways. At times, it felt like I was in a dark tunnel searching for a glimpse of light that was nowhere to be found. There were other moments when a crashing wave jostled me about, causing me to have to regain balance. There also were occasions when it seemed like a torrential down pour chilled my bones and forced me to find ways to warm myself. Most common was the roller coaster ride with twists, turns and nosedives that dizzied me. There was no choice but to stop, get hold of myself and take some time to regain focus. All of these played out at one time or another in what became a tug of war challenge in which I felt pushed and pulled with unforgiving strength. Because of geographic distance from family, these 'grief behaviors' seemed all the more intense. After withstanding them for a number of months, often being reduced to a puddle of tears, I knew I could not nor did I have to walk on the road of grief by myself, but I realized it would have to be my choice, my decision to find productive, supportive and positive ways of coping.

What emerged as a daily repetition of wrenching sadness became the catalyst for seeking the guidance of Dr. Michael Cristiano, a clinical psychologist. During early sessions, I dreaded sitting with him not only because there were so many questions but also because tears often spoke louder than words. How do I bear this loss? What more could I have done? What 'red flags' did I miss? How will I ever find myself and be able to move forward? These questions, causing my head to spin, would prove not to have easy answers or provide quick relief from the gut-wrenching pain that squeezed and twisted my heart. The process was slow, often tedious. There were times when it seemed as though I never would glimpse a light at the end of that tunnel.

Occasionally, my therapist would say, "You are right where you're suppose to be." At first, I interpreted these words as some form of clinical analysis intended to evaluate my position on my journey. That was not the case at all. I came to understand that those words meant that wherever I was on my road and however I felt as I walked its path was right and perfect for me. They were intended to guide me as I wrestled with my emotions at any given point in my travel. As time passed, I felt more able to convey my emotions and seemed more capable of getting a grip on this life circumstance. I came to realize that the journey of grieving is not linear; it does not move in a straight path. The imagery of the tunnel, crashing waves, heavy rain and the roller coaster made sense for the first time. I understood that grieving does not follow rules or abide by set formularies. It intrudes when and as it wishes, sometimes with a gentle nudge and, at others, with a full-blown punch in the gut.

It took quite a while, but there did come better days. I treasured those hoping they would last but, as way goes on to way, the reality played out differently. They were fleeting and caused me to wonder if my mind was playing tricks on me by providing these pleasant yet short-lived thoughts and images. Then I would see, hear or read something that triggered the sadness. These moments were sometimes so overwhelming, I began to think I was regressing, moving in reverse on my road. Slowly, I became more adept at negotiating my way through the rocky, unsettling emotional episodes. As they became fewer, with a longer period of time between them, I came to grasp and become more comfortable with a key characteristic of the grieving process. Time was not an adversary; it was becoming my friend.

In conjunction with Dr. Cristiano's help, the core of my homework was to address my personal spirituality. I needed to take the beliefs housed in my mind and move them into my heart. I needed to go to peace and not continue to go to pieces. I needed and wanted to experience the gifts of joy and happiness once again. I needed to reflect deeply on words I had heard so often, "Golgotha (death) does not get the last word." With even greater resolve, I had to focus on the more positive, profound significance of resurrection — the experience of new beginnings, hope and possibilities all of which were centered in my understanding of omnipresence.

With this intentional recentering came a clearer lens of perception. Love cannot die, so what John and I shared still lives. It lives in my mind and heart, indeed, in every fiber of my being. Each time I pause to remember him, I feel surrounded by his spirit. This awareness evolved into an 'epiphany' moment during a therapy session well into my journey and has been an empowering force in my forward movement. Dr. Crisitiano said, "As much of John as could be taken away has been taken away." These words were perplexing to me at first because I was clueless about what they meant. After grappling with what I thought was a strange notion, I came to recognize that although John is no longer with me in a physical sense, all that we shared together never can be taken from me. All the blessings of our togetherness in life are mine to keep. The myriad memories of twenty eight years of a beautiful relationship belong to me. No one or nothing can separate me from all that is mine to cherish. This was the turning point that moved me further away from the pain and accompanying inner turmoil to a conscious refocusing on remembrance. It has become a great gift in my life.

This ability to remember and truly 'own' all that was **us** has allowed me to smile more and cry less. These sacred instances became more meaningful when I assumed the role of Minister of Pastoral Care and was invited to co-lead a bereavement group at my church, working alongside my supervisor, Rev. Anne Atwell. Because of these opportunities, I have been blessed with greater awareness and ever-evolving understanding. I have felt an inner strengthening which has opened me to listen to and identify in some ways with the journey of others as well as welcome the subtle ways by which community has been built. I have heard the pain of many who grieve and have seen visible sadness. But I have also witnessed growth and for some, a new-found appreciation for their sense of confidence and purpose. These women and men have allowed me to enter upon the roads on which they journey. They have stirred in me a depth of compassion greater than I realized was within me. They have enlivened my spirit with hope and have been instrumental in helping me to place sadness in its proper place...situated where newness obscures the potential for on-going damage this force is capable of inflicting.

I have become convinced that the root of my grief at its beginning was fear. This was the unseen force that created self-doubt, a sense of helplessness, and a pervasive loneliness that, for a time, seemed impossible to conquer. As a result, fear as the agent of doubt, helplessness and loneliness came to occupy much of my praying and reflecting. I find that it has taken on a more positive 'persona' in my life as I dwell on its challenge: Face Everything And Rise.

A particular gospel narrative has become quite meaningful to me because it speaks to the experience of fear that comes from loss, and the invitation to rise above it:

> John 20.19-22 (The Message, adapted)
>
> *...the disciples had gathered together, but, fearful of the Religious authorities, had locked all the doors in the house. Jesus entered, stood among them, and said, "Peace to you." Then he showed them his hands and side. The disciples, seeing the Teacher with their own eyes, were exuberant. Jesus repeated his greeting: "Peace to you. Just as I was sent, I send you." Then he took a deep breath and breathed on them. "Receive the Holy Spirit," he said.*

This brief story illustrates how fear is capable of guiding thinking and behavior, but it also highlights the potential for change and growth. Just as the friends of Jesus were fearful and felt compelled to hide behind locked doors after his death, that is how I felt once the reality of John's passing set in. I locked away inside myself the me I once knew because I was fearful about things which, until then, had been commonplace in our life together. I felt as if part of me also had died, and I was terrified. I just wanted to hide from the indescribable, unthinkable reality that changed life in what seemed like the blink of an eye. I realize, now, just as much as wanting to hide from things external, I was needing to hide from myself. But there is good news! Jesus becomes present to those huddled in that place and offers a greeting of peace...twice. Then he tells his friends that they are to continue the work he began. As if to give his dear ones a second wind, he takes a deep breath, breaths on them and imparts words of empowerment.

The predicament of the disciples mirrors my circumstance, and what has come from reflecting on this particular scenario is a source of encouragement and strength. It is a reminder that I am never alone, never forgotten, never abandoned. I am reassured that I possess within me all I need to move forward as I imagine, hope for and trust in the possibilities that might be. As the disciples came to realize that neither were they broken nor was there a need to submit themselves to paralyzing fear, I am refreshed and invigorated. Those gathered were able to unlock the doors, come out from their fear and be about the business of life. It was a moment of transformation in which they were able to put Golgotha in its proper perspective and reclaim life with newness and hope. In those moments of spiritual connection with Jesus, they experienced a shift in perception and understanding and, in a very real way, they were witness to their own personal resurrection.

As the power of healing does its sacred work in my life, changes continue to occur. In the past they were slow, sometimes with undetectable presence, but these have become more evident as I journey on my road. In my thoughts, words and actions, I recognize an earnest desire for on-going growth. While I remain a traveler on the path of my experience of loss, I am keenly aware of the need to seek and embrace those interior dispositions which will affirm, enrich and continue to nurture newness in my life. Although there do occur tender moments sometimes accompanied by tears, these come less from the weight of sadness than an ever-deepening sense of gratitude that comes from remembering John. Because of the profound significance and far-reaching effects of this great blessing, I share the following imagery as a transition to the next body of writings in this work:

> *"It is this gift, securely housed in consciousness and comfortably situated in the seat of emotions, which invites me to walk through a portal. Beyond it, I find myself in a familiar place, joined by my dear one. In that realm, alive with vibrant images and pleasing impressions, I recreate a portrait of his sterling personhood which fills me, once again, with great admiration. At the same time, glimpses of the beautiful life we enjoyed flash before me and cause my heart to become consumed with deep affection."*

The Treasure Chest

II

"Remembering the good times you shared keeps the one you lost in your heart long after they are gone. At first, reminders are a salt in your wound, but the great moments you had together will start to seep back into your heart after your fears slow down some. When sadness isn't the first thing that hits you one morning, maybe then there will be room for remembering."

Carol Wiseman

We all share a common wealth. It may not be in the realm of material possessions or financial assets, but is very real and available to us whenever we wish to tap into it. It is unseen by anyone but ourselves because it exists in the inner sanctum of the mind. It is the holder of those precious gems we call memories. It may take some time for us to go to this treasure chest but eventually, when we feel ready, willing and able to unlock it, we might find that its contents are a source of sustenance that enables us to recollect and relive not only times of special significance shared with our loved one but also the beauty that was 'the miracle of ordinary days.'

I am blessed to have had past opportunities to put into writing so much of what occupies space in my special treasure chest. As meaningful as were these sentiments when written between 2006 and 2009, they are ever-relevant today and have taken on a greater and deeper importance. Some of them are excerpted from my poetic trilogy which include: *In the House of the Father*, *The Looking Glass*, and *Voice of a Different Heart*. Non-fictional references are cited individually.

It is my hope that your heart will be touched by something you read, either in this section or the ones that follow it, and provide some inner strengthening. Perhaps one particular writing, maybe more, will speak to you and draw you into the sentiments being expressed because you find connection with them. May this sharing encourage you to go to the special place within that is yours alone to savor and gift you with a measure of peace.

Coming to Realize

You are the fantasy
Of every yesterday
I did not know.
Yet, looking for you relentlessly,
I had no doubt you were waiting
Somewhere between morning and night.

You are the reality
Of each today,
No longer existing in vagueness,
So much more than imagining
Or hope could reveal,
Allowing me, at last,
To forget that endless exploration.

You are the hope
Of all tomorrows:
Joy of dawn's light
Awakening that which once slept
In numb fear
And bosom of evening's rest,
Cradling me in the harbor of safety.

Rx for Two

I promise to respect and affirm you –

Appreciating and embracing your uniqueness,
Knowing that we will not always agree,
Celebrating your gifts, talents and interests,
Understanding that times of forgiveness are inevitable,
Striving, always, to be kind, sensitive and generous.

I promise to love you –

When sadness or uncertainty surround you,
When you are happy being with family and friends,
When we are alone in moments of quiet peace,
When, each time I look at you,
I remember our beginning and smile,
When each new day greets us and we continue …
   Together and forever.

For A Greater Purpose

I look beyond **me**
And make a choice for us
Because the equation is fact,
That two are greater than one.

I place above **myself**
What creates all of we
Because its strength in oneness
Gives fullness to twoness.

I gift love's **I**
To the whole of its our
Because the union of two
Gives richness to one.

Essence

During our journey of life together, John and I were the beneficiaries of a variety of learnings and lessons about the nature of relationship. These came from the day-to-day homework of being intentional about nurturing its rhythm and movement. Our perceptions became strong beliefs that found expression as we lived them. Not only did they fill us with affirmation during times of happiness and great joy but also guided and supported us when we faced circumstances which were challenging:

> *True loves does not demand conformity, for to impose it is to smother potential. Rather, it seeks to enliven and enrich individuality. That is when emotions can be revealed as true expressions of freedom and equality.*
>
> *The dazzling jewels in the crown of commitment are loyalty and love. The former is a gift of the spirit; the latter, one of the heart. Neither can thrive unless given freely and unconditionally.*

Blueprint

No amount of wishing
Can make for a happy union,
But some hope for survival exists
If common sense joins reason
And understanding's spirit
Aligns with priority's oneness.

No more than white on white,
Construction's vacant blueprint
Remains absent of identity
Until hand in hand
And heart to heart
The new design is conceived.

Emotional investment
Is the one, sure foundation
On which rests emerging vision,
Then desire births potential
Which gains both form and substance
And the plan reveals definition.

Only sturdy bolts and braces
Will hold the structure in place
And if open communication
With needed compromise
Are the tools of common choice,
More likely it is to endure.

Abiding as its protector,
The roof is placed, at last,
And if insulated very well
With unconditional love,
It will stand a vigilant sentinel
That safeguards blueprint's fruit.

Tradition

Compelling us to make more from less
In those early days
Of austere living,
The season bid us welcome
So we might again experience
That wondrous merriment
Of past knowings.
We wanted, needed it so
To visit us
And stay for a time.
Thoughts of tradition
Had a taste
No more than bittersweet,
As we held close the images
Of years gone by
But now vanished
Except for remembrance.

The excitement of our children,
With faces of innocent belief
And breathless anticipation,
Were with us still
As this decking of the halls
Spoke few words
But screamed emotions
Which tried to release lament.
He and I were alone
In this web of irony
Trying to recreate
An aura of festivity
In the midst of squeezing sadness.
The charm of this joy
In other lives which had lived
Was at rest forever,
As we faced material nothingness
In this place of newness.

Afterglow

That first tree was massive
With freshly cut scent
Which filled the room
And labored to distract us
From the daily reality,
The skeleton of sparseness
With notice of all things
Borrowed or second-hand.
Despite the apparent monotony,
Which was inescapable
On cursory glance
And had arisen
From circumstances, not desire,
This glad greenery of nature
Spoke our vision,
The hope of its gentle presence
With arms outstretched
To embrace us and gift peace.

F. L. Richards

The glittering top
And a few ornaments
Faded from overuse
Are the happy survivors
Of two decades of display,
And as each year
Since their first exposition,
They look into our hearts
And quietly remind us
That we should never forget.
Others have been more lavish
But we promise them faithfully,
These red and gold treasures,
While staring into their history,
That there will never be another
Standing in that same humble grandeur,
Possessing such modest eloquence,
Impossible to recreate.

Shadows of Daylight

In the shadows
Of daylight's reflection
Are revealed on pavement
The forms of two
Who walk together.

The outlines are concrete,
More than just an impression
Open to subjective bantering
Which is able to misrepresent
What vision clearly defines.

There is no place to hide
From an unspoken declaration
About the nature and substance
Of what closeness wears
As it journeys forward.

F. L. Richards

Ministry of the Street

There is something quite special about planning a trip, especially in a new relationship like ours was in 1986. Our senses were awakened to possibilities as we considered location and how long would be our stay. Once we agreed upon a place for our initial venture, John and I became filled with anticipation, allowing our imaginings to go to work. The routine of responsibilities and obligations would be placed on the back burner for a time as we considered how awesome it was going to be to indulge in some 'self-pampering.' We looked forward to becoming acquainted with as many particular characteristics of our destination as possible. We trusted that these experiences would be sources of making new memories.

Some of the plans we made would become a reality. Unknown to us, however, was a very different type of exploration which would arise from the unexpected and contain a larger than life element of surprise. The following is an excerpt from the book we co-authored, *Dark Streets, Bright Lights,* and describes how the unforeseen evolved into beautiful blessings and rich, enduring memories:

Puerto Rico is affectionately called Isla Del Encanto, Enchanted Island. Its lushness, intense sun, inviting waters and prolific flora, home to the indigenous tree frog, the coquí, are testaments to its captivating beauty and charm. The geography of the island exudes a charisma that is inescapable, and the distinctiveness of its cultural character entices and intoxicates those caught in the web of this tropical paradise. This is how it was for us during our very first vacation together in the summer of 1987.

We became immersed in this euphoric atmosphere and were drawn back, again and again, to savor more of what had been our first taste of delight. That initial swallow of sweetness took on a different flavor during what evolved as an uninterrupted era of almost thirteen years. It changed to one that was bittersweet as we became wrapped up in the lives of many who, under normal circumstances, would have remained unknown to us. Some worked the streets; others just worked. All tried to make life more bearable in a common goal of survival. It wasn't easy for them, especially those who chose to make something of their lives which extended beyond the immediate, the here and now. The others seemed incapable of thinking outside the perimeter of the present because that was all they knew.

We never could have imagined that we would come to find ourselves inside the bubble of such an unlikely togetherness or how these individuals, each and together, would affect us from a variety of life perspectives. Our hope for all of them was two-fold. We longed for them to come to understand the meaning of unconditional kindness and generosity of spirit. More importantly, we wanted the gift of self-worth to be found, once again, by those who had lost sight of it, and strengthened in others for whom it was a shrouded abstraction as circumstances dictated.

Like so many who come from a different reality than theirs, we might have sat in judgment of need and want, and the varying degrees of turmoil visible in all. We chose another route which John's brother, Richard, called "the ministry of the street." For a variety of reasons, they were fragile souls wanting to be looked upon with understanding, and wounded spirits needing to be listened to with compassion. (pp. ix, xii)

We never considered any token of kindness to be extraordinary. Guided by compassion manifested in hospitality, we followed the urgings of our hearts by reaching out to those who, by many, were considered "the least among us." What became indelibly imprinted in us was the uniqueness of each one's presence with its candor, respect, moments of evident vulnerability, smiles, tears and heartfelt words of gratitude.

This experience of being on the island was transforming. Our relationship with twelve men and women stirred us from complacency, challenged us to abandon comfort even at times when it would have been easier to step away, and compelled us to view life from a very different perspective. John and I discovered how similar were our spiritual attitudes and that we were living them together. It enriched our relationship and added a depth of closeness unknown to us in the past.

The lessons and learnings were many, varied and some quite unusual. From this span of time, we developed a personal 'credo,' a statement of belief that came to guide decisions and the actions which followed during the remainder of our years together:

> *"Before any of us may claim the possession of a caring nature, we do well to consider that...a truly generous spirit takes on substance and flesh...when there is a willingness to embrace the struggle of another human being."*
>
> p. xiii (adapted)

It is Enough

Side by side,
Clinging to the heart and spirit
Of the other
When there was nothing else
To grasp hold of,
We have walked together
These many years.

Through all the seasons
Of a life truly blessed,
We have answered the call,
Straightforward and unafraid,
Making this oneness
Stronger, deeper, more passionate.

Unhampered by attachments which divide,
Causing double vision,
It is enough, this luxurious simplicity,
Making singular the embrace
Of essence and being,
Inviting new closeness,
Unknown even yesterday.

Renewal

I see with the eyes
Of a panoramic spectrum
Because you have opened them
To a wide vision of life's landscape.

I listen with the ears
Of an innocent youth
Because you have taught them
The songs of simple beauty.

I walk with the spirit
Of an enlivened confidence
Because you have shown it
That distance cannot deter.

I soar with the wings
Of an exploring bird
Because you have challenged them
To fly toward new discoveries.

I rejoice with the words
Of an exultant hymn
Because you have sung that melody
To my starving soul.

I rest with the heart
Of wholeness and gratitude
Because you have given it
The greatest of all gifts.

Turkey Day

Of all the special occasions during the year, Thanksgiving had a special significance to John. He was steadfast in his desire to honor and respect its purpose and was very intentional about detaching it from what seemed to be the months old attention given to Christmas. The philosophy was simple. It was a day on which to gather with those close to us, enjoy a wonderful meal and just allow conversation to flow. It was a day of thanks on which to focus and reflect about the many blessings in our lives, but it was also an opportunity to reach out and be giving to those we had come to know who were less fortunate, particularly those who were homeless. It became a joy-filled, yearly tradition for him to prepare enough food so that we could enable these folks to enjoy the day as they were able.

It always was heartwarming to observe smiles on the faces of the nine women and men at 'the camp' as boxes of food were unpacked and arranged on a plastic table. From that very first occasion, it became a ritual for us to stand with them and join hands in prayer. For all of the years this very small community existed, we shared some of our bounty with them, and they blessed us not only with expressions of gratitude, but also just by being who they were. Spending some time with these friends on this day of remembrance enlivened us and made our gathering at home all the more meaningful.

Vivid in my memory as I recount it in my book, *Crossroads... Journey to Wholeness*, is this special day in 2001, our first Thanksgiving after moving from Puerto Rico to Florida:

The Thanksgiving dinner table seems to be a forum for reminiscence. It was no less true of our gathering. Most of us being 'older' spoke about some health issues laced with humor. I laughed as I remembered family celebrations years ago when this topic consumed the conversation and sparked the annoyance of us younger people. One of our guests asked John about his experience with heart surgery in 1995. My eyes filled with tears because the image was as sharp as if it happened recently.

Coffee and desert provided a transition from the serious to the humorous. People seem fascinated when we retell the scenarios and sagas of our life together. I chuckled and said three words, 'the money can'. John's smile erupted into laughter, and our guests wanted to be let in on what was obviously a private joke. We kept our household funds in a small can bearing a safe-like facade. Despite our professional positions and salaries, we lived from check to check. Putting extra money aside for our personal needs was a challenge. Because we had growing children with needs, buying a pair of shoes became a luxury.

Noting our comfortable home, there would come the inevitable question, "How did you survive?" The comment I provided for our guests was one that spoke to the deep belief we have always valued..."I wouldn't care if we had to live in a mud hut. As long as we're together, that's all that has ever mattered." We have learned that our commitment has been shaped by the who of our relationship and not the what, and has been a repeated testament that what we share is as good as it gets. The connecting of looks between the two of us was one of those incredible moments in which the noise of conversation faded and our souls touched. It was a sacred instant that added to an already perfect day. (pp. 210-213 (adapted)*Second printing*, ©2008)

Christmas Again

Because you love me
I have no need or want,
Yet Christmas revisits me
With each new rising
As I awaken with eagerness
And unwrap, once again,
The greatest of all gifts.

It is never twice the same
In bright, stunning appearance,
As fresh paper and bow
Excite my child-like spirit,
And the vision which lies within
Gives new meaning and purpose
To the plan of our journey.

Warm Reminder

I gaze upon your face
And wonder what fortune
Was mine in our meeting.

I listen to your gentle words
And think how nurturing
Are their sounds in my ears.

I feel your consuming love
And cling ever-tightly
To its enlivening power.

I rejoice in our life together
And remember that moment
When courage was the victor.

Imprint

The texture of your skin,
The shape of your eyebrows,
The blue pools which are your eyes,
The fine, light silk which is your hair,
The sensitive strength in your hands,
The warmth of your consuming arms ...
    I must remember them.

The sound of your voice when speaking,
The melodies of your heart in song,
The laughter that tickles my soul,
The whispers of quiet intimacy,
The shouts of excitement or surprise,
The sighs of compassion for another's pain ...
    I must remember them.

The gift of your gentle humility,
The spirit of your indomitable kindness,
The golden heart that beats inside you,
The purpose and plan of our life,
The blessing of this unique relationship,
The inseparable togetherness of many years ...
    I must remember them.

Yes, I must remember them all,
Because life will change one day;
We feel the transitions
Already taking place.
And if God should call you first,
A thought I cannot bear to consider,
I know, within the reality
Of the yesterdays and todays,
That each tomorrow shall be filled
With these images, etched forever,
Within the broken monument
Of my longing heart.

Night's Gift

The curtain is drawn
Upon a day now ended.
In my weariness and longing,
I need to feel your presence
And absorb your gentle smile.
I look to no one but you,
For no other knows the way
To relieve the tension
And soothe my tired spirit.

You are my cradle of peace,
Harbor of sure safety,
Not just desire of sunlit hours
But evening's darkening drape.
You, alone, can ease all ills
As you nestle me closely
And invite sleep to come,
Tucking me, yet again,
Inside the heart of my heart.

Interplay

Beyond the field of dreams
And the realm of fantasy
Lies a reality,
An essence, a depth
Which whispers in softness
and echoes with affirmation.
Obscured by the challenge
Of confounding chaos,
It becomes visible
In the tranquility
Of sublime stillness.
Worn as a cloak,
It is a reminder
Of its powerful
And protective presence:
Once discovered...tightly held,
Once experienced...forever treasured.

Afterglow

Listen for its urgings,
Welcome refreshment
For the soul.
Be open to its cheers,
Joy givers to the substance
Of wholeness.
Look for it, giving embrace,
Letting it envelop you,
Your shield and support,
The only enduring sustenance.
Hold fast to its core,
Posturing naked honesty
And complete abandon.
Be not deterred
By the negativity
Of its antithesis,
But empowered
by the well-spring
Of its life - giving force...
It is love!

Crossroads...Journey to Wholeness
F. L. Richards © 2008, second printing
pp. 271-272

The Present Reality

of

Time and Place

III

"Losing someone we love is an initiation. Our life changes. It is not going to be the same again. All our relations with other people and ourselves are forced to shift. We become a new person. Although a part of our heart breaks, the spirit of the departed remains. Through that spirit, love continues to flow, helping to show us the way, if we allow it, to lighter states of grace and wisdom we were born to reach."

Sobonfu Somé
Emerging from the Heartache of Loss, Carol Wiseman,
"Acceptance...Moving forward at last" pg. 89

I have become more and more aware that the experience of loss and grief is inseparable from the larger picture of life. That is because there is a seamless connection between the past and present, what was and what is. During times when I felt overwhelmed and emotionally exhausted, I attempted to repress and ignore thoughts and feelings that were intimately bound to both. As much as I wanted the anguish to go away, I came to realize that those instances when I did not want to confront grief did not deter it. I learned that if I was unwilling to acknowledge its presence, it would confront me and demand a response. It became all too obvious that I needed to adjust my lens of perception. That involved a conscious shifting away from avoidance to a posture of being fully present during every occasion of sadness, regardless of how intensely I might be affected. This was an important lesson that equipped me to move through the pain, get to the peace and accept an undeniable reality...life does go on.

Although the previous description speaks to my journey, it illustrates that there is a location along the way that is a common meeting place for all who grieve. We eventually come to a crossroad where an important decision must be made. We may remain stuck in the quick sand of past sadness and heartache, or lift ourselves from its forceful hold as we become open to changes in our thinking, what we say and how we behave. No matter how great or small, obvious or subtle, any degree of newness we recognize and are willing to own becomes a testament to growth and some measure of healing.

The remaining writings describe where I now find myself on my path. Some allude to the past only as a segue to the here and now...the todays of my life. The connecting of these realities enables me to create a wholeness, a unity, a sense of continuity that I find comforting, and this bridging affords me continued opportunities to place more into my storehouse of hidden treasures.

Faith

I go to the glassy reflector
Wanting it to speak to me
In words which explain,
Making sense of the abstraction.
I ponder in protracted stare,
Wondering when I will see something
Which gives definition and shape,
Making it tangible.
I search inside what I know
Thinking therein lies a substance
Which will invite my touching,
Giving description to its texture.
I lapse into a moment of rest,
Choosing sounds of silence
Over the nothingness set before me,
And come to realize
That it alludes all senses
Wanting simply,
That I believe and trust.

In the Beginning

All of the 'firsts' after a loved one has died take on a marked change in personality. Holidays and special occasions like birthdays and anniversaries tug at heart strings as we think back to past celebrations. They may be approached by developing expectations with which we saddle ourselves, or we may allow ourselves to simply be in each moment as we are able, while searching for a way to negotiate our way through them and attempt to hold on to a thought or mental photo that will encourage us to be gentle with ourselves.

I found it difficult to consider the word, celebrate, because the wound of loss was so fresh and raw. I faced a 'trifecta' of these days that occurred within two weeks of John's passing. His birthday, the day we had set aside to remember the beginning of our journey together and Valentine's Day appeared and the best I could do was to cope with getting through them. I spent a great deal of time at the cemetery because it was the place I felt closest to him. Combining periods of silence with attempting to express emotions and watering the grass with my tears seemed to be the ritual of each visit. On those days, 'connection' was especially important not only with John but with his children. Reaching out to them was a way for all of us to remember the particular day and share a oneness as we felt their dad's presence. These times were also an ever-present reminder to me that I was not the only one grieving this loss. Those special moments placed us all on the same road and helped to mask the pain a bit because we were keenly aware that we were not alone; we had each other.

During the first year, connection occurred frequently. On the 29th of each month, we were intentional about communicating with each other. With each time of togetherness, by text or phone, there were signs of gaining some perspective that resulted in gradual shifts in conversation. These were empowering moments because I realized that geography was not an obstacle but an opportunity to experience closeness and enable all of us to feel some inner changes.

The importance of connecting became evident, also, during times when family and friends visited. During the month of March my sister, Margaret, spent some time with me. Ordinarily, she is a 'get up and go' kind of gal, but this visit was different. She was sensitive to my needs and was content to move at a much slower pace. The visit to the cemetery was her first. I do not ever recall her being as visibly emotional as she was in that moment. She expressed sentiments that were beautiful and heartfelt, but not surprising, because she had developed a close relationship with John during our years together.

In October, she visited again. This time she was with Dennis, my brother-in-law. I was happy because I knew this stay would be more vacation-like for 'Mags.' The pace of activity was sure to speed up considerably. There was another cemetery visit, this time a first for Dennis. I do not remember his exact words, but I was touched by his expression of affection for John. Apparently, his being at the cemetery prompted a desire to reminisce once we returned home. During a visit to us years earlier, he made plans to golf. When he awakened that morning at 5:30, he found John at the stove. Surprised, Dennis asked him why he was up so early. John responded, "You can't go out without having a good breakfast." Dennis was deeply affected by John's concern and spirit of hospitality because this retelling became part of many conversations during subsequent family gatherings. Other than these moments of serious reflection, I believe that they were intentional about keeping our time together light and lively. It was just that, including their 'baby wipes' incident that resulted in my having to contact a plumber. This was the first time since my loss that tears came from laughing and not from sadness.

The most challenging time during that year was the holiday season. As much as I wanted to ignore these weeks beginning with Thanksgiving, my mind was alive with the imagery of what had become our traditions, especially those of Christmas Eve. Church, eggnog, our favorite music and the exchanging of gifts had been our way of celebrating for all the years we had shared life. That first Christmas Eve, I insured that the hours would be occupied by requesting roles at our three church services. At least this would make time pass and allow me to put aside what was so painful to remember. Just from the exhaustion of so many hours, I'd be able to return home and get some rest. Surprising to me was the inner calm I felt as I opened the front door. This sustained me during those next hours of sleep.

Then there was Christmas Day and that next week to move through. I knew I would be supported by Rocco, his friend Gonzalo, and Caroline, who made a trip to Florida because they did not want me to be alone for my birthday or the day after, which was New Year's Eve. This most generous gesture proved to be more positive than I anticipated. Their presence and affection were truly gifts of indescribable value, freely given and accepted by me with immeasurable gratitude. There was also some mutuality during our days together because we all felt John's presence strongly.

Afterglow

Thinking back to the gifts of 'presence' I received during that difficult first year, I have come to believe that, each and together, they were subtle seeds of healing that were being planted and which, at some point, would take root and grow in my consciousness. Although I could not recognize it then, I realize now that I was so blessed to have been surrounded by such love and support.

Not Devoid of Life

Our home is minus one, but not devoid of life. It expresses itself in spirit which penetrates and soothes my being. I hear the sounds of his footsteps, the ritual of his greeting each day, "Good morning, sunshine," his whistling and humming which sometimes erupts into accompanying an operatic aria. I see his face, gentle and smiling, relaxing in his favorite chair, sometimes reading, at others in moments of conversation with me. I feel his presence, not as an abstract image or figment of imagination but in ways that are real, tangible and touch my very essence. Yes, our home is minus one, but not devoid of life. John will always be with me in this private world, this place of tranquility that, together, we labored to build.

Let There Be Light

During the winter of 2012, what began as the simple task of reupholstering the love seat in our family room became a major remodeling project. The existing Gone With the Wind museum-like appearance would be transformed into a contemporary setting. All of the statuary, collectible plates, books, posters and pictures that festooned that space for years were packed and given to John's son, Michael, who once had voiced an interest in the items. The new look was more in keeping with other rooms in the house. We invested in Scandinavian teak furniture and chose lighting and wall accents which complimented it.

There was one piece of furniture, however, which stood apart from the rest. Diagonally positioned in the far end of the room is a double glass door display cabinet with interior lighting. In it is housed special glassware and small crystal figures and other mementos purchased by us in our travels. Often, we sat together in that room at night, the only lighting emanating from that cabinet. It was during those special moments that we relaxed in the peaceful atmosphere and talked. I loved being there with John, observing an obvious look of contentment on his face.

At times when our attention was drawn to the keepsakes, our minds became filled with heartwarming images of the past. We spoke of cruises taken with our friends Ray, Bud, Tony and Bob. These afforded opportunities to explore islands south of Puerto Rico and learn about their rich history and culture. We often reminisced about our more than twenty five years of close friendship with Charles and Bill. During that span of time, they lived in three different homes in New England. Our visits to each of them were eagerly anticipated because of their gracious hospitality. We remembered how those times together were filled with laughter and a seeming child-like merriment. We fondly recounted vacations with them to Spain, San Francisco and our many adventures in Provincetown. Whenever we spoke about this special group, we were reminded of how each and together, their friendship was interwoven in the fabric of our life journey.

That room remains appealing, but being in it is now different. It is a quiet affair absent of conversation but not memories and the emotions stirred by them. I continue to revisit parts of our life that sit on the shelves of that cabinet, but each inward gaze is bittersweet. Most of these precious ones who filled our life with joy are gone. Each encounter is accompanied not only by thinking back but also with a prayer of gratitude for the unique ways we were enriched by their presence. May Bill, Ray, Bud and Bob rest in light eternal.

A beautiful source for remembrance, that cabinet has taken on an even greater importance. Not long after John's passing, I came home one evening and noticed that the lights were on. I thought nothing of it and assumed that I had forgotten to shut them off. But then it occurred to me that I didn't recall turning them on. Months later, this happened again and there have been similar occurrences as time has passed. There is no electrical shortage which might be a plausible explanation, nor is any other furniture nearby which might hit the cabinet causing the lights to shine.

Deep within the heart of my spirituality, I trust that these on-going occurrences are not coincidental. I firmly believe that the spirit lives on because it is of God, part of God. Therefore, it is impossible to separate it from the Divine, which is everywhere present. I have always felt John's spirit close to me in our home. Some how, some way, his energy is in that light. Such a thought has been amazingly comforting to me, especially when I experienced overwhelming emotional weakness. Despite the skepticism of others with whom I have shared this story, I continue to hope for and trust in what the light has come to mean to me. It is times like these that I am strengthened and can feel more and more healing happening. And God said, "Let there be light." I echo that sentiment. May it always be so!

Revelation

Filtering through thick, ominous clouds,
Faint glimpses of what once was
Become visible but then pulled away
As if the need to play hide and seek
Is a cruel joke that prevents discerning,
Despising the need to identify a fleeting image,
Encased, again, before it might be recognized.

Like sentinels that blanket the sky
Withholding warmth that might have soothed
The chill of piercing sadness, these insidious ones,
Tricksters to their core, are masterful
In their unspoken declaration of opposition
And fueled by apparent and unapproved control
As they render abstract the deep desire of the heart.

"Could this be yet more unmet longing?",
I ask myself one day as I gaze upward
And witness the birthing of a new dawn.
I linger and watch rays, held hostage till now,
Push through the guardians of the dome
And as if with unapologetic, undeterred resolve,
Light reclaims its rightful place and purpose.

Transition

Nature's movement experiences a rite of passage as it departs from the color-filled, brisk days of autumn. Trees are barren and absent of life. Serenades that once filled the air from within thick canopies no longer are audible. The blanket becomes stark white, icy cold, and puts to rest the green blades that lie beneath it. It is a time of marked quiet but not an ending.

One morning, perhaps unnoticed to some at the onset, birds resume their melodious songs, buds are visible as trees awaken from their slumber, and newness emerges from the soil. There is no rhyme or reason that might explain the precise day or time of these occurrences, this visible transformation, but it does happen. Life returns and continues onward.

Sorting Things Out

When I began my grief journey, I really was not aware of the variety of challenges I would face. Almost immediately, the internal discord of emotions became evident and held me in a vice-like grip. All that was going on inside me dictated my behavior. It seemed that no two days were alike, and such unpredictability was not comfortable for me. I remember trying to out-guess and out-smart my internal workings, but that was an exercise in futility. I felt and reacted accordingly. I saw no other way to function than to allow myself to go with the flow of feelings as I negotiated my way 'one day at a time.' It was a disconcerting process but one which demanded attention.

In conjunction with being an emotional mess, it occurred to me that there was another process which would need consideration. The difference was that this one was external, visible. It involved going through John's clothing and personal possessions and deciding what to do with them. There emerged a strong, very evident connection between this task and what was going on in the realm of what guided thinking and feeling. I equated parting with what belonged to him as an admission of the reality of loss. That acknowledgment meant that I was letting go, and I just could not face what was an inconceivable possibility. The emotional voice within me was relentless in reasoning that as long as John's clothes hung with mine in two closets, part of him was still there. Many times, too many to count, I wrapped my arms around his shirts and wailed as I smelled the lingering aroma of his cologne. It was a seeming validation that I should not remove anything. The fragrance coupled with my ability to visualize him in various garments cemented my impression that, as long as I was able to experience these moments of closeness and comfort, there was no need or desire to attend to the task of 'sorting things out.'

Earlier in my writing, I mentioned that I came to realize that time was not an adversary but a friend I recognized, more and more, as an ally. With its passing, my perspective changed. John's presence was not based solely upon the external, what was concrete and revealed through my senses. I came to a more profound realization that it was securely housed in my mind and heart. His presence was an internal stirring always at my disposal. My ability to embrace this deepening belief was the catalyst that enabled me to make the decision which I had avoided for twenty one months.

In October, 2015 during a visit from my friend, Rocco, who had been an important part of our life together since its beginning in 1986, I postured my thinking to him. It was time! He stood with me as I gazed at John's clothing one last time. Removing the garments individually, I held each close to my heart then folded and bagged them for pick up by a local organization to which we had contributed clothing and household items in the past. A few dress and tee shirts were placed aside for John's son, Michael, who once asked if he might be given some of his dad's favorites. On the scheduled day, I placed three bags on the front porch just as the truck pulled up. The driver walked toward and greeted me, but I could not acknowledge him with words; I just waved. Before he could scoop up the bags, I leaned over and placed my hand on each one. I felt like I was encased in silence and in that moment, I felt John's presence.

This task was a valuable learning experience for me. Despite the well-intentioned urgings of others to 'get it over with,' I confronted the chore of 'sorting out' in my own time and when I was ready, willing and able to accomplish it. What I initially had perceived as a daunting obstacle that would intensify my sadness was actually a blessed opportunity to reassess 'presence' in a more positive way. It was no longer solely dependent upon things tangible but how it existed in the home of the unseen, the internal, the invisible arena where matters of the heart reside. Becoming emotionally stronger has gifted me with a greater clarity of perception and understanding that has resulted in an unshakeable reassurance. Although many of John's physical possessions are no longer with me, spirit continues to exist. The strength of connection we had shared in life has not ended; it has changed in form and substance. I realize that the letting go of material things does not mean that I have let go of him. I have come to rely more on the experience of John's ever-present spirit that expresses itself in many ways. It is in those beautiful moments, those sacred instances, that I feel surrounded by rays of hope and beacons of light which, I am convinced, will guide and sustain me during all the days of my life.

In the Midst of Silence

Away from the noise of life
I go to the silence,
That place of risky comfort,
Unsure of reason or destination.

I open myself to impressions
Which could be black and white,
Stark absolutes in the pages of memory
Of what was in decades past.

Subtle changes transform the photos
Bearing color more varied and beautiful,
Giving sharper, more pleasing focus
To the journey that was ours to share.

In that refreshing garden of remembrance
I remain for as long as I will,
Allowing pleasant sensations to affirm
That, now and always, John is part of me.

Then and Now

When a loved dies, we experience a whirlwind of emotions which may render us incapable of clear thinking and feeling. In this fragile state, we become susceptible to second-guessing and uncertainty about so much of what had been the norm, the routine of life as we knew it. In part, that is because of the presence of the insidious intruder called doubt. It unforgivingly seeks to rearrange pictures while replacing calm with chaos. It is unconcerned with permission as it causes disconcerting echoes from tireless hammering. Its work is that of thievery, obscuring the authentic self and holding fast to vulnerability with relentless effort. It believes its place is one of dominance in the unyielding quest of making less of what once was more.

When John transitioned, I vividly remember my daughter, Jennifer, holding me close as I sobbed, "I can't do this...I don't know how to do this alone." Maintaining a steady posture she responded, "Dad, you are strong; you can do this!" In that moment, I felt the depth of her love, but those words rang hollow because I truly did not believe I was equipped for anything beyond the present reality of death. Doubt already had made an appearance and was at work. Everything was muddled and confusing. The very thought of self-reliance made me shake. The idea that all was now up to me made me want to recoil from that prospect. All that I knew in our life together blurred into indiscernible images. I felt as if I was in a wilderness not knowing which way to go or, for that matter, where I was heading.

While praying one evening many months after the funeral service and burial, I became distracted by a thought which interfered with concentration. "We are the creators of our own possibilities." It seemed odd that this particular statement would visit my consciousness at that very moment. These words were familiar to me. I had heard them during course work and homilies a number of times. Possibilities? What are they? How do I go about embracing abstract notions? There were questions, but the answers were elusive. As out of reach as they seemed, something within me compelled a closer study.

As the reminder settled into in my thinking and I worked through the muck of grief, I slowly became capable of grasping hold of what was both an invitation and a challenge. I came to understand that, indeed, this was the response to doubt that would allow me to release it. There was no quick remedy or overnight transformation. My work was two-fold. It included being and doing...being open and receptive to the idea of new possibilities and doing the work necessary to incorporate them in my life. In truth, I was unsteady for a time but the more I considered and reflected, the greater became my resolve to move out from feeling the emotional captivity engendered by doubt to one of internal liberation that was accompanied by improved vision about what might be.

There came a time when those words took on a different and deeper significance with images more positive and life-giving. Almost a mantra-like reflection, I have committed myself to the truth that, indeed, I am the creator of my own possibilities. What was once an idea shrouded in vagueness has evolved into a learning that is embedded in my living. It truly has been this change in perception that has positively influenced my emotional stability. I accept what I cannot change, but I will not acknowledge doubt as a squatter who lets the weight of its ponderous baggage clutter and consume space in the home of my being.

In Search of Answers

In my role as co-facilitator of a bereavement group, I have found that some participants, especially those whose experience of loss is relatively recent, are filled with many questions. A number of those whose loss was sudden are intent on grappling with inquiry that focuses on "What if?". Discussions have revealed that these can be a heavy burden and add a significant amount of anxiety to an already stress-filled situation.

I know well that I cannot provide answers to others because I, too, wrestled with many questions when I began my journey. What I am able to express, however, are thoughts which have helped to lighten the weight of my grief and enable me to give greater concentration to a more positive, powerful idea:

> *"I have come to realize that the journey of grieving is not about questioning myself because of what might have changed the outcome. Rather than being consumed with mourning the loss of relationship, I choose to feel thankful and blessed that we lived it."*
>
> F.L. Richards

The Tie That Binds

    The image of concentric circles,
        a tri-unity invited with gratitude
    fills the void and floats in consciousness.
        As I consider this powerful, life-giving presence,
    I drift into the realm of its significance
        in this place on the road of healing.

    I am bound with inseparable connection
        to the God of my understanding,
    the fullness of omnipresent love and
        source of unconditional relationship
    that echoes from the seat of perception
        and becomes outwardly manifested.

    I am joined to the one who no longer
        journeys with me, yet his presence
    is real, a tangible testament to all
        the yesterdays and every today of living,
    neither having been diminished by physical absence,
        but infused with a new substance of meaning
            that recreates the gift.

I am surrounded by those precious
    in my life who impart affirmation
and encouragement which uplifts, nurtures,
    strengthens and motivates the search
for moments of epiphany which reveal
    new and different understandings.

I am filled by each and all, these catalysts
    that guide me to embrace eager movement
on the uncharted path of the road before me
    to the here and there of every tomorrow.
The core of abundance, alive within my 'allness',
    clings to abiding love, the tie that binds.

Empty Tomb

I came out,
Leaving behind
The bindings,
Placing the pain
On the floor of that darkness
In which it had resided.

I came out,
Leaving the torturous existence
Inside
Where it would wander
No more.

I came out,
Looking to the day,
Rolling the stone
Once and for all
Across the night.

> "Just as I am in this time and place of my being, I am filled with gratitude for a life shared, a love experienced, and even for the journey that has forever changed but not ended them. And so I affirm that hope and healing, comfort and courage continue to be gifts available to me. As I embrace them, I look to each tomorrow alive with possibilities and abounding with blessings on their way to me."
>
> F. L. Richards

Guideposts...

Thoughts and Reflections

for the Journey

IV

"Words are powerful conveyors of meaning and purpose. Sometimes, however, they escape expression because we are unable to articulate them. During times such as these, we may rely on the wisdom of others to shed light on the road before us."

F. L. Richards

It has been quite clear that during the early stages of grieving, my thinking was scattered and my emotions were fragmented. This was the internal forum in which I understood and interpreted words, and it was this place of turmoil from which I attempted to articulate what I was feeling. As well-intentioned as they were, some people in my life were attached to the 'you should, must, have to' syndrome believing that what they were voicing was useful, productive advice. Quite to the contrary, that was not the reality. At times, I found myself feeling impatient with others who believed they were helping me by providing a seeming time line for my journey. It was impossible for them or anyone to grasp my experience of the loss of one with whom I shared many years of life and love. My ability to express myself with even minimal clarity was obstructed by a dynamic which only I could fully understand. Often, words failed me and for a while, I felt a sense of ineptness, one of seeming verbal incompetence.

I have found that the statements of wisdom which follow helped me to work through the myriad dimensions of loss and grief. They served as aides which enabled me to formulate thoughts I frequently was unable to express. Comfort was the primary goal for examining them. As perceptions and emotions have undergone palpable changes, I view these statements in a different light. They remain comforting, but they now provide a feeling of reassurance that is empowering. As I examine them with a new intentional focus, I am able to recast the imagery tucked inside the words and find a deeper, more profound significance and a depth of truth I could not grasp hold of earlier. Each and together, these invite and challenge me to understand their purpose with ever-growing inner strength.

"The reality is that you will grieve forever. You will not 'get over' the loss of a loved one; you will learn to live with it. You will heal and you will rebuild yourself around the loss you have suffered. You will be whole again but you will never be the same. Nor should you be the same nor should you want to."

Elisabeth Kubler-Ross

"You are my God: all good things come from you...you give me all I need...and so I am thankful and glad and I feel secure."

Psalm 16:2,5,9

"Ego says, 'Once everything falls into place, I'll feel peace.' Spirit says, 'Find your peace and then everything will fall into place.' "

Marianne Williamson

"Trusting that God is with you is comforting. You can rely on the God of your understanding when the picture of your life gets blurred...you only need to be still long enough to hear that small voice within: I am with you."

Carol Wiseman (adapted)

"It's not forgetting that heals. It's remembering."

Amy Greener

"Oh God, you have let me pass the day in peace; let me pass the night in peace. Under your hand, I pass the night. You are my Mother and Father...Amen."

Traditional Boran (African) Prayer

"I will try to let the weight of guilt and regret slip away...I am loved and love makes all kinds of allowances -- and keeps on loving."

Martha Whitmore Hickman

"In the middle of winter I at last discovered there was within me an invincible summer."

Albert Camus

"God is my shepherd; I shall not want. God lets me lie down in green pastures and leads me beside still waters. God restores my soul... so I will not fear, for God is with me."

Psalm 23:1-4 (adapted)

> "No person, no place, and no thing has any power over us, for we are the only thinkers in our mind. When we create peace and harmony and balance in our minds, we will find it in our lives."
>
> Louise Hay

> "You are braver than you believe, and stronger than you seem, and smarter than you think."
>
> Pooh's Great Adventure

> "As I lie in bed, I remember you...because you have always been my help. In the shadow of your wings...I cling to you and your hand keeps me safe."
>
> Psalm 63:6-8

"Grief is not a condition to be cured but a natural part of life. Spirit does not know loss. It knows that every story begins and every story ends, yet love is eternal."

>   Louise Hay and David Kessler

"God is my shelter and strength...So I will not be afraid...God is with me."

>   Psalm 46:1,2,7 (adapted)

"We do not have to rely on memories to recapture the spirit of those we have loved and lost -- they live within our souls in some perfect sanctuary which even death cannot destroy."

>   Nat Witcomb

Final Thoughts

As I think back and reflect, I am reminded that "It takes a village to raise a child." I believe this statement bears truth as it relates to my journey of loss, grief and healing. The 'community' in my life has nurtured and helped me to grow. Their ever-present love and support, demonstrated in many and varied ways, has encouraged me to be authentic as I worked through the multi-layered dynamics of a very challenging, painful circumstance. What emerged was a gradual emotional strengthening that enabled me to feel more and more grounded. Companion to that process, the decision to revisit the richness of my relationship with John enabled me to view the gifts of gratitude and renewal from a broader perspective of meaning and relevance that was positive and productive. Together, these interior dispositions influenced an understanding of healing in ways that were real, true and honest for me.

Beyond the scope of my journey and the writings related to it, I have found it both useful and necessary to be intentional about giving consideration to 'others.' That involved being conscious of and attuned to the ways in which the contents of this work might be affirming for our families and friends, any person who may be grieving a loss, and those who share that individual's life.

It is my hope that those in our circle of family and friends might use the sentiments expressed in this book as a guide that encourages them to gaze inward and unlock their own special 'treasure chests.' Although different and unique for each of them, the contents are the same. They consist of the 'gems' of vivid images, special memories and heartwarming emotions. By allowing themselves to revisit times of joy, happiness, celebration, laughter and contentment, may they be blessed with the riches of that precious gift called remembrance.

For any who are in the midst of sadness that comes from the loss of a dear one, no matter how recent or long-standing, my prayer is that this reading has been a source of reassurance that the process of grieving is not a 'one size fits all' journey that is based upon a prescribed time line or a list of expectations that is absolute. Every moment of travel is right and perfect because no one else can comprehend the magnitude of another's personal loss. Whether a conscious thought or not, each step taken on the road of this experience speaks to courage and the commitment to want to move forward. Most importantly, especially during moments that are tumultuous and seem overwhelming and unbearable, may those who mourn, hear the gentle whispers of their loved one reminding them, "As I loved you in life, that love remains. You are not alone."

Mindful of the importance of so many in my life, it is essential to emphasize how vital and valuable is the role of others in the experience of one who grieves and attempts to figure out what a 'new normal' is all about. Family members and friends who may find themselves in that position have a beautiful opportunity. By being available and demonstrating a steadfast closeness, the gift of connection is offered. This may help to alleviate a feeling of isolation, the sting of loneliness, and the confusion of so many different emotions vying for attention at the same time. The one who is ready and willing to accept the generous gestures of those who are part of their lives may, in time, experience a gradual shift in their thoughts and emotions. In part, that is because they have received the blessings of presence, compassion and affirmation.

Indeed, this labor of love is finished but my journey continues. It exists in a place that is beyond the acute pain of loss and grief. It is a place where new understandings are waiting to be discovered, new possibilities are waiting to be experienced, and new joys are waiting to be embraced. To be open and receptive to these gifts of life does not require me to place my dear one aside. Rather, I am invited into newness as I carry John with me, his ever-living presence worn as a mantle that enfolds me with the warmth of abiding love. As I venture forward, I feel a strong sense of anticipation when I consider the profound words of film actor, Patrick Swayze:

> *"When those you love die, the best you can do is to honor their spirit for as long as you live. You make a commitment that you're going to take whatever lesson that person was trying to teach you, and you make it true in your own life. It's a positive way to keep their spirit alive in the world...by keeping it alive in yourself."*
>
> *And so it is!*

A Special Remembrance

As I completed the writing of this book, a difficult but necessary decision had to be made. No longer having a quality of life that would sustain him, Rico, our pet companion, was put to rest. His manner with all people was warm and friendly. His ability to cause laughter with his unique antics was uncanny. The love he shared with us was unconditional. His very presence gave great joy to our days and in the years since John's passing, Rico was a source of comfort to me. About him, John often said, "He is the best pet we ever had." How true are these words!

July 27, 2006 — August 13, 2016

About the Author

F.L. Richards was raised and educated in New York. He earned undergraduate, graduate and post-graduate degrees from Queens College, Hunter College and Pace University. During his career in the field of education, he worked as a teacher of Language Arts, administrative assistant, assistant principal and principal.

In addition to serving as an ordained deacon and Minister of Pastoral Care at his church, he has engaged in studies at the Samaritan Institute, its educational arm. In 2012, he earned a Master of Religious Studies degree and currently is a candidate for the degree of Doctor of Divinity.

Richards is an associate member of the Academy of American Poets. His passion for writing encouraged him to offer classes to seniors in his home community. An important focus is his outreach to the homeless in his neighborhood. Other interests include music, theater and travel.

During the decades of journeying with his partner, John, there was a simple principle which guided, nurtured and sustained their relationship:

> *"It is not important who*
> *you love but that you love...*
> *unconditionally."*

Other works by F. L. Richards

Non-Fiction (Autobiographical)

Crossroads....Journey to Wholeness

Poetic Trilogy

In the House of the Father

The Looking Glass

Voice of a Different Heart

Non-Fiction (with Steve Brunner)

Dark Streets, Bright Lights....
The hustlers, homeless and hopefuls of Puerto Rico

Available at Amazon.com
and www.FideliPublishing.com

www.ingramcontent.com/pod-product-compliance
Lightning Source LLC
Chambersburg PA
CBHW061223070526
44584CB00029B/3957